Expressions
of the
Heart

**A little book
to inspire your heart**

mpiled by **Barbara Laporte**   *Original artwork by* **Donna Bennett**

Published by HeartLifter Publications
www.heartlifters.com

Design by Amy Kirkpatrick
Typography and production by Dorie McClelland
Printed in Canada

ISBN: 978-0-9764183-1-3

Scripture passages from Luke, Proverbs, and Ezekiel taken from
THE MESSAGE. Copyright © 1993, 1994, 1995, 1996, 2000,
2001, 2002. Used with permission of NavPress Publishing Group.

Other scripture passages taken from the Holy Bible, NEW
INTERNATIONAL VERSION®. Copyright © 1973, 1978, 1984
International Bible Society. All rights reserved throughout the
world. Used with permission of International Bible Society.

The publisher gratefully acknowledges the websites brainyquote.
com, coolquotes.com, gagirl.com, heartquotes.net, honeymoons.
about.com, poetseers.com, thekindcards.org, thinkexist.com, and
worldofquotes.com for the remaining quotations.

Introduction

Hearts, a symbol of love, became especially symbolic to me after the death of my husband. On many occasions, I would feel *dis*heartened, and just when I needed it most, I would find a heart-shaped rock or shell, and felt as though he was letting me know that all was well. Inevitably, I was comforted and encouraged by these symbols of his love.

It occurred to me that perhaps I could use hearts to send a message of comfort and encouragement to others, and what better way than to compile quotations from some of the world's great thinkers? It was great fun to research quotations that included the word "heart" and even more fun to convince my dear friend Donna Bennett to embrace her inner artist and see how her inspirational illustrations fit with the quotes that I found. Like our friendship, the book evolved over time, and it is our sincere heart's desire that you, your friends, and family find the artwork and quotations in this little book uplifting.

Heart-felt blessings,
Barb Laporte

Expressions of the Heart

Go to your bosom;

Knock there,

and ask your heart

what it doth know . . .

Shakespeare

Wheresoever you go,

Go with all your heart

Confucius

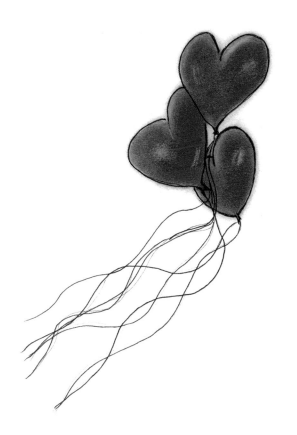

You are rich, though

you do not know it.

You have wells of kindness

within your heart.

Kabak BaMishol Hatazar

. . . seed(s) in the good earth—

. . . are the good hearts

who hold on no matter what,

sticking with it until there's a harvest.

Luke 8:15

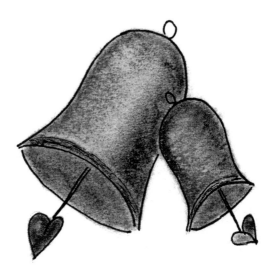

Love from a pure heart,

a good conscience,

and a sincere faith.

1 Timothy 1:5

The heart that loves

is always young.

Greek Proverb

Glory in his holy name,

Let the hearts of those

Who seek the Lord rejoice.

1 Chronicles 16:10

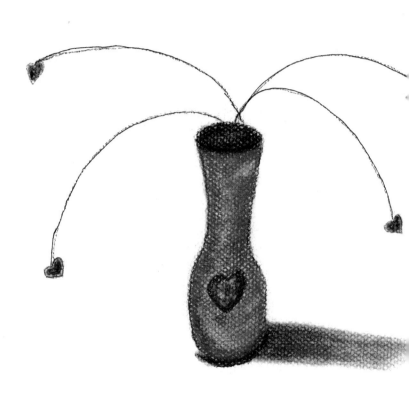

Find the seed at the bottom

of your heart

and bring forth a flower.

Shigenori Kameoka

Trust God

from the bottom of your heart;

don't try to figure out everything

on your own.

Proverbs 3:5

A part of you has grown in me,

together forever we shall be,

never apart, maybe in distance,

but not in heart.

unknown

The only lasting beauty

is the beauty of the heart.

Rumi

The thousand mysteries around us

would not trouble us,

if only we had

cheerful, healthy hearts.

Nietzche

For it is the God who said,

"Let light shine out of darkness"

who has shone in our hearts . . .

2 Corinthians 4:6

What would we do with these gifts?

Give of your hands to serve

and your hearts to love.

Mother Teresa

My heart is steadfast;

I will sing and make music.

Psalms 57:7

Just as water mirrors your face,

so your face mirrors your heart.

Proverbs 27:19

Take delight in the Lord,

and he will give you

the desires of your heart.

Psalms 37:4

I will give you a new heart,

and put a new spirit in you . . .

Ezekiel 36: 26–27

Those who do not know how to weep with their whole heart don't know how to laugh either.

Golda Meier

Peace I give to you...

Do not let your hearts be troubled,

do not let them be afraid.

John 14:27

Be patient toward all

that is unresolved in your heart

and try to love

the questions themselves.

Rilke

A kind heart is a fountain of gladness,

making everything in its vicinity

freshen into smiles.

Washington Irving

Song brings of itself

a cheerfulness

that wakes the

heart of joy.

Euripides

There is no harvest

for the heart alone;

The seed of love must be

Eternally Resown.

Anne Morrow Lindbergh

Keep love in your heart . . .

The consciousness of loving and being loved

brings a warmth and a richness to life

that nothing else can bring.

Oscar Wilde